PHYLLIS J. LE PEAU & NCF STAFF

THE
CHARA
—OF—
CARING
PEOPLE

*8 Studies for Groups
or Individuals*
With Notes for Leaders

CARING PEOPLE BIBLE STUDIES

INTERVARSITY PRESS
DOWNERS GROVE, ILLINOIS, USA
LEICESTER, ENGLAND

InterVarsity Press, USA, is the book-publishing division of InterVarsity Christian Fellowship, a student movement active on campus at hundreds of universities, colleges and schools of nursing in the United States of America, and a member movement of the International Fellowship of Evangelical Students. For information about local and regional activities, write Public Relations Dept., InterVarsity Christian Fellowship, 6400 Schroeder Rd., P.O. Box 7895, Madison, WI 53707-7895.

Inter-Varsity Press, UK, is the book-publishing division of the Universities and Colleges Christian Fellowship (formerly the Inter-Varsity Fellowship), a student movement linking Christian Unions in universities and colleges throughout the United Kingdom and the Republic of Ireland, and a member movement of the International Fellowship of Evangelical Students. For information about local and national activities write to UCCF, 38 De Montfort Street, Leicester LE1 7GP.

Some of the studies in this guide are adapted from material originally written by Nurses Christian Fellowship staff.

Cover photograph: Michael Goss

USA ISBN 0-8308-1197-4
UK ISBN 0-85111-336-2

Printed in the United States of America

15	14	13	12	11	10	9	8	7	6	5	4	3	2	1
03	02	01	00	99	98	97	96	95	94	93	92	91		

Getting the Most from
Caring People Bible Studies

Caring People Bible Studies are designed to show how God equips us to help others who are in need. They reveal what the Bible has to say about the pain we will all face in life and what we can do to care for friends, family, neighbors and even strangers who experience pain.

The passages you will study will be thought-provoking, challenging, inspiring and practical. They will show you how to focus on others, but they will also help you focus on yourself. Why? Because these guides are not designed merely to convince you of the truthfulness of some idea. Rather, they are intended to allow biblical truths to renew your heart and mind.

These Bible studies are inductive rather than deductive. In other words, the author will lead us to discover what the Bible says about a particular topic through a series of questions rather than simply telling us what she believes. Therefore, the studies are thought-provoking. They help us to think about the meaning of the passage so that we can truly understand what the biblical writer intended to say.

Additionally, these studies are personal. At the end of each study, you'll be given an opportunity to make a commitment to respond. And you will find guidance for prayer as well. Finally, these studies are versatile. They are designed for student, professional, neighborhood and/or church groups. They are also effective for individual study.

How They're Put Together
Caring People Bible Studies have a distinctive format. Each study takes about forty-five minutes in a group setting or thirty minutes in personal study—

unless you choose to take more time. The guides have a workbook format with space for writing responses to each question. This is ideal for personal study and allows group members to prepare in advance for the discussion. At the end of the guides are some notes for leaders. They describe how to lead a group discussion, give helpful tips on group dynamics, suggest ways to deal with problems which may arise during the discussion, and provide additional background information on certain questions. With such helps, someone with little or no experience can lead an effective study.

Suggestions for Individual Study

1. As you begin the study, pray that God will help you understand and apply the passages to your life. Pray that he will show you what kinds of action he would have you take as a result of your time of study.

2. In your first session take time to read the introduction to the entire study. This will orient you to the subject at hand and the author's goals for the studies.

3. Read the short introduction to the study.

4. Read and reread the suggested Bible passage to familiarize yourself with it.

5. A good modern translation of the Bible, rather than the King James Version or a paraphrase, will give you the most help. The New International Version, the New American Standard Bible and the Revised Standard Version are all recommended. However, the questions in this guide are based on the New International Version.

6. Use the space provided to respond to the questions. This will help you express your understanding of the passage clearly.

7. It might be good to have a Bible dictionary handy. Use it to look up any unfamiliar words, names or places.

8. Take time with the final question in each study to commit yourself to action and/or a change in attitude.

Suggestions for Group Study

1. Come to the study prepared. Follow the suggestions for individual study mentioned above. You will find that careful preparation will greatly enrich

your time spent in group discussion.

2. Be willing to participate in the discussion. The leader of your group will not be lecturing. Instead, he or she will be encouraging the members of the group to discuss what they have learned. The leader will be asking the questions that are found in this guide.

3. Stick to the topic being discussed. Your answers should be based on the verses which are the focus of the discussion and not on outside authorities such as commentaries or speakers.

4. Be sensitive to the other members of the group. Listen attentively when they describe what they have learned. You may be surprised by their insights! When possible, link what you say to the comments of others. Also, be affirming whenever you can. This will encourage some of the more hesitant members of the group to participate.

5. Be careful not to dominate the discussion. We are sometimes so eager to express our thoughts that we leave too little opportunity for others to respond. By all means participate! But allow others to also.

6. Expect God to teach you through the passage being discussed and through the other members of the group. Pray that you will have an enjoyable and profitable time together, but also that as a result of the study, you will find ways that you can take action individually and/or as a group.

7. We recommend that groups follow a few basic guidelines, and that these guidelines be read at the beginning of the first session. The guidelines, which you may wish to adapt to your situation, are:

☐ Anything said in the group is considered confidential and will not be discussed outside the group unless specific permission is given to do so.

☐ We will provide time for each person present to talk if he or she feels comfortable doing so.

☐ We will talk about ourselves and our own situations, avoiding conversation about other people.

☐ We will listen attentively to each other.

☐ We will be very cautious about giving advice.

☐ We will pray for each other.

8. If you are the group leader, you will find additional suggestions at the back of the guide.

Introducing the Character of Caring People

There was a time in my life when I was in crisis, agonizing over the pain of a broken friendship. It was one of the darkest periods of my life. What made it worse was that I knew I had caused the trouble. I was disobedient to God. I refused to forgive someone who had hurt me deeply. I withdrew from people because I was not willing to risk any further hurt.

One friend, Marj, responded by praying for me faithfully even though she was a target of my anger. It was years before she saw God's answer to her prayers in my life and in our relationship. But Marj kept praying the whole time. This has had a lasting effect on me.

Another person, Rose, was "just there" during that time. She communicated hope when I felt hopeless by spending time with me. Occasionally, Rose encouraged me by gently speaking thoughts from Scripture about God and his character. She believed God for me when my faith ebbed low. I was loved and accepted when I knew that I did not deserve to be. There was no way that I was earning love at that time in my life.

God used caring people to make himself known to me and indeed to bring back light into a very dark life. Because of friends who stuck by me and encouraged me, I have grown.

There were people around us who opened their homes to our children and took care of them when I was *very* pregnant (I was never *just* pregnant, you understand—always *very* pregnant) and down with a bad back. Sometimes they showed up on our doorstep with a meal. Their generosity was a special gift to us in this time of need. There are others who help keep our marriage alive and well by entertaining our children for a weekend or more so that my husband and I can focus on each other and our relationship without interruption.

Everyone needs care. Every one of us is a victim of the consequences of sin. Broken childhoods, hurting marriages, lonely widows, left-out minorities. We are surrounded by needy people.

Sadly, it doesn't stop "out there" in the world. There are many unmet needs among Christians. A friend recently told me that it was evangelical Christians who made it clear that they did not want a minority family in their neighborhood.

Even in our local congregations there are many people who do not *feel* cared for. One family I know went to a church looking for fellowship and left after a year, needs unmet. They felt they could not survive there any longer. No one reached out to them. Nobody invited them to their homes. Few even bothered to introduce themselves and welcome them. People were too busy to care.

Then there are some who are working desperately at home and in foreign lands doing the work of God who feel isolated and unsupported, close to burnout, because they are denied the support and care of other people.

Christians who have gone through divorce, who are single parents or who simply never married have told me often how they feel like unwanted, out-of-place misfits in our marriage-oriented churches.

Sometimes the church is guilty of not loving as Jesus has called us to love because of plain indifference. We need to recognize that we are a called people. We are called by God to care. But many times it is simply that people who really want to care for others don't know how. The studies in this guide will help you get started. While looking at these specific character qualities, we begin to understand how God develops character in us. At the same time we will recognize our limits—only God is God in people's lives.

This study guide is for people who want to know and respond to what Scripture says about how to continue to grow as caring people.

1/Called to Care

Isaiah 61:1-3

Many people in the world are in pain. They are hurting spiritually, emotionally and physically. I don't have to go outside my own neighborhood or church to feel their agony. At times I wonder how I can possibly make a difference.

What would happen if each of us took the call to minister in Christ's name seriously and did his or her share? For instance, statistics tell us that if Christians gave just one-tenth of their income to the work of God, there would be no financial needs in Christian work. Wouldn't it be the same if believers did their share of caring in other ways? If we each did our parts, most, if not all, of the physical, emotional and spiritual needs would be cared for.

1. Who in your life has cared for you?

2. Read Isaiah 61:1-3. In Luke 4:17-20 Jesus read this passage in the synagogue and then said, "Today, this scripture is fulfilled in your hearing." To whom was Jesus called to minister?

What was he to do?

3. As disciples of Jesus his call to minister to others becomes ours. Who are the "brokenhearted," the "captives" or the "mourning" in your life?

4. What is involved in binding up someone who is brokenhearted?

How do we proclaim freedom to the captives?

What does it mean to comfort those who mourn?

5. How do you feel about being called to this kind of ministry?

6. The images in verse 3 are not commonly used today. But what do these three vivid sets of contrasts communicate to you about the results of caring for others?

7. What do you think the author is trying to communicate through the image *oaks of righteousness?*

8. How can we care for people in a way that sees beyond their imperfections to what God wants them to become?

9. Think of one person—a family member, a friend—who needs your care. What can you do for that person according to this passage?

10. What might the end results be in his or her life? (Be specific.)

Ask God to use you in that person's life. Pray for his or her release, healing and growth, asking that God will ultimately display his splendor in the person's life.

2/Faith
Genesis 22:1-19

My heart responded with emotion. My eyes with tears. I listened to the words that were sung by a choir of orphans from Uganda. The African beat to their music was catchy and happy. Their eyes were bright. Their hearts were filled with joy evident by what and how they sang. They knew Jesus and, in spite of the pain and loss they had experienced on earth, they sang with conviction, "Some day soon we are going to see the King, and there'll be no dying there." What a vivid demonstration of faith as "being sure of what we hope for and certain of what we do not see" (Heb 11:1). Those children believed God.

1. When have you felt that your faith was inadequate for what God called you to do?

2. Read Genesis 22:1-19. When God calls Abraham's name, he responds, "Here I am." This shows Abraham's readiness for obedience to God. When

is your attitude toward God like Abraham's?

When is it different?

3. What feelings and questions do you think Abraham had as he listened to God's instructions and proceeded to obey?

4. According to Hebrews 11, faith is "being sure of what we hope for and certain of what we do not see." What evidence do you see throughout this passage of Abraham's faith?

5. Abraham said to Isaac, "God *himself* will provide the lamb for the burnt offering." His faith was based on who God is. What did Abraham learn about God through this experience?

6. What is the relationship between faith and obedience in this passage?

7. What is the relationship between obedience and caring for others?

8. What happened because Abraham obeyed and believed God (vv. 12-18)?

9. Sometimes when caring for people in need, it is difficult to be "certain of what you do not see." In what relationship are you having difficulty with this? Why?

10. In what ways, if any, has looking at Abraham affected your outlook in that situation?

11. Abraham saw his son spared and a sacrifice provided. Why is it important for us to expect to see God doing things *now* as well as in the future?

12. How were others affected by Abraham's faith (vv. 15-18)?

What difference can it make in a needy friend's life that you are a person
of faith?

*Pray that God will increase your vision of who he is, thereby increasing your
faith and making your attitude toward him what he wants it to be.*

3/Hope
Colossians 1:15-29

S ome days I feel no need to hope for the future because things seem so good now. The children are happy and healthy. Relationships are especially alive and satisfying. The sun is shining. God seems near.

Other days I feel blue, a bit depressed. My energy is low. Growth and change seem to come very slowly, or not at all. And then there are the days when life may not seem worth living. The heavens are like brass. It seems like every person in my life is in pain. There are unmet needs everywhere I glance. This is the kind of day in which being a person of hope seems very difficult.

---

1. What makes you feel discouraged?

---

2. Read Colossians 1:15-29. What does *supreme* mean?

Identify the ways that Christ is supreme according to this passage.

3. What does it mean that Jesus "is the image of the invisible God" and that all of God's "fulness dwells in him"?

How are you affected by this fact?

4. Often people feel discouraged because they feel like their world is falling apart. What is significant about the fact that in Jesus "all things hold together" (v. 17)?

5. What does it mean that Jesus is the "firstborn from among the dead" (v. 18)?

How should this truth about Jesus affect the way we relate to someone facing death?

6. Verse 21 speaks about alienation from God. How do you see this alienation from God demonstrated in the world around you?

7. Because of who Jesus is, what is he able to do for us (vv. 17-22)?

How do you respond to this?

8. Because of what he believed, Paul was full of hope. How did this affect the way he served others (vv. 24-29)?

9. How are you affected by someone who is genuinely full of hope?

10. When are you full of hope?

11. Hope, like love, is seen in our actions. What actions can you take this week toward someone in need to reflect the hope that is in you?

Ask God to express through you the "hope of the gospel" this week.

4/Love
Luke 10:25-42

He was a very popular speaker. His books and articles touched many people in the evangelical community. His ability to think through difficult issues was impressive. But there was one bold truth that stood out during his memorial service that day as people shared how they had been affected by this man's life. Joe Bayly *loved* people! When people talked, they did not mention his books or his speaking or his mental ability. They simply told of the acts and words of love that had flowed from his life to theirs. As a result of his love and care, they had been exposed to God's love; they had been healed, redeemed and given hope.

---

1. How do you usually feel and respond when you see someone suffering?

What if it is someone you don't know?

2. Read Luke 10:25-42. In this passage an expert in the law tests Jesus by asking, "What must I do to inherit eternal life?" How does Jesus answer his question (vv. 26-28)?

3. What do we learn about the lawyer in verses 25-29?

4. How are you like the lawyer, and how are you different?

5. The robbers, priests and Samaritan encountered the wounded man. What might have motivated the action of each toward him?

6. What motivates you to serve others?

7. Look at the Samaritan's actions one by one. How does each act demonstrate love?

8. How is the Samaritan obeying the law quoted in verse 27?

9. In verses 38-42 do you identify with Mary or Martha? Why?

10. When Martha complains, Jesus responds that Mary has chosen what is needed. What do you think he meant?

11. What is communicated to people when we act "worried and upset about many things"?

12. What is communicated when we are still and listen?

13. As we review this passage, we see that both the Samaritan and Mary both showed love, but in different ways. How would you describe the difference?

How could you show love to someone this week like the Samaritan did?

How could you show love to someone this week like Mary did?

Ask God to help you show love to that person, making you sensitive to his or her specific needs. Ask him to help you be still and listen to Christ so that you can know his love and love others.

5/Generosity
2 Corinthians 9:6-15

P overty was widespread among Christians from the mother church in Jerusalem. This stemmed from Jewish believers being cut off from relatives, society, employment and the temple at the moment of their conversion.

Paul challenged the church at Corinth to become involved with the needs of their brothers and sisters and to express their loving concern through generous financial giving. In doing so he provides us with two chapters (2 Corinthians 8—9) on the philosophy of Christian giving.

1. What is it easiest for you to be generous with? (time, money, material possessions or your family?) Explain.

2. Read 2 Corinthians 9:6-15. One of the principles of Christian giving is give what you have decided in your heart to give. Why is "intentional" giving necessary for Christians?

3. Why do you think that the attitude we have in giving is as important as the gift itself (v. 7)?

4. When are you most apt to struggle with a reluctant spirit in relationship to giving?

5. Describe God's involvement in the life of the giver as it is seen in verses 8-11.

6. When have you experienced God's grace abounding to you as you have been involved in giving to others (such as your own needs being met [v. 10] and/or being able to meet others' needs that you thought you wouldn't be able to [v. 11])?

7. Besides God's involvement in our giving, what are the other consequences of generous giving (vv. 12-14)?

8. How is verse 13 an example of "putting your money where your mouth is"?

9. According to verses 12-14, what are the results of your gifts?

How do you respond to this?

10. In what ways do you struggle with giving to others generously?

11. What from this passage motivates you to give generously?

12. What do you need to do to become a person who gives more generously?

This powerful passage on Christian giving ends with the words, "Thanks be to God for his indescribable gift!" Ask God to make the reality of this marvelous gift so vivid to you that generous giving to others becomes a natural outflow of it.

6/Encouragement
Hebrews 10:19-25

Thank you, Miss Skriba, for encouraging me," says a seven-year-old brown-eyed boy to his grade-school principal.

Encouragement does not go unnoticed.

The way I play volleyball is dramatically affected by the attitude of my team members. I have had the best brought out of me and made plays that I didn't think I could make when positive and hopeful words came from my teammates. I have also been somewhat paralyzed on the volleyball court at those rare times when members of my team have come down hard on my mistakes.

If this is the case with a seven-year-old grade-school student and an adult on the volleyball court, it makes encouragement in the Christian life very important. The writer of Hebrews is on target when he says, "but let us encourage one another."

---

1. Describe the last time that you were encouraged by someone in any way.

2. Read Hebrews 10:19-25. According to verses 19-23, what is the confidence we have?

Why do we have that confidence?

3. Compare and contrast your usual response to someone with whom your conscience is clear to that with someone you have hurt or offended and it has not been made right.

4. What should our response to God be (v. 22)?

5. What do you think it means to "hold unswervingly to the hope we profess"?

6. What instructions are given in verses 24-25?

7. How does hope and God's faithfulness affect your ability to spur others on to love and good works and to encourage them?

8. How have you been encouraged by another in your walk with God?

9. Why is meeting together as Christians important when it comes to encouraging one another?

10. What makes such times with other Christians encouraging?

11. What are ways you can think of that would encourage others in their walk with God?

12. As you think about the people that you are called to care for, why is being a person of encouragement important?

13. What steps do you need to take this week to become a more encouraging person?

Ask God to make the fact that "the Day" is approaching a reality to you. Pray that you will grow as a person of encouragement.

7/Hospitality
1 Peter 4:7-11

I have many happy memories from my days of growing up. One that continues to have a long-term effect on me is the "open home and heart" policy that my folks lived out. Not only did they open our *home* to college students, their friends, their kids' friends and to people who needed a place to live, but they opened their *hearts* to these people at the same time.

It is this hospitality, I think, that the Scriptures speak of in this passage.

1. What do you usually think of when you hear the word *hospitality*?

2. Read 1 Peter 4:7-11. List the instructions that Peter gives to Christians in this passage.

3. Why should the fact that "the end of all things is near" motivate Christians to obey these instructions?

4. What does a clear head and self-control have to do with praying?

5. How do you think prayer is related to loving each other deeply (v. 8)?

6. How does offering hospitality to one another seem to be a natural outcome of loving each other deeply?

7. Describe specific ways of practicing hospitality.

8. Why do you think there is a special warning about "grumbling" when it comes to hospitality (v. 9)?

9. What enables you to extend hospitality without grumbling?

10. How have you experienced God's grace being administered to you through receiving hospitality?

11. In this passage we are called to serve faithfully, administering God's grace to others. Why is it important that a caring person be a person of hospitality?

12. What help is offered to you in this passage (vv. 7, 11)?

13. Who in your life is in need of experiencing God's grace through your hospitality?

The outcome of offering hospitality in the strength of God is that God will be praised through Jesus Christ. Pray that God will give you the strength to reach out to the people in your life who need your hospitality.

8/Accepting Our Limits
Exodus 18:13-24

I f there is any way that God has been working in my life over the past months, it is vividly demonstrating to me my own limits. This has been painful. It has also been good. I am not God in my friends' lives. I cannot bring about healing or change. I cannot force a person to perceive truth. Only God can do these things. I can be faithful and humbly wait for God to do the rest.

1. Would you describe yourself as an underachiever or an overachiever? Why?

2. Read Exodus 18:13-24. Describe Moses' job.

3. What is Moses' father-in-law like, according to this passage?

4. What might Moses have been feeling at this point in his life?

5. In what ways do you identify with Moses in verses 13-16?

6. How was Moses' father-in-law used by God in Moses' life?

7. In what ways have you come to know your limits when caring for others?

8. How do you respond to the realization that you have reached your limits?

9. How have people in your life been helpful in this process? (How easy or difficult is it for you to listen and respond to the counsel of other wise and caring Christians in this area?)

10. What were the benefits of Moses acknowledging and accepting his own limits?

11. What are ways that you can evaluate what you are doing and whether you have reached or surpassed your own limits?

12. What benefits can you see happening in your life if you acknowledge and accept your limits?

Ask God to give you wisdom concerning your own limits and how to grow in acknowledging and accepting them.

Leader's Notes

Leading a Bible discussion can be an enjoyable and rewarding experience. But it can also be intimidating—especially if you've never done it before. If this is how you feel, you're in good company.

When God asked Moses to lead the Israelites out of Egypt, he replied, "O Lord, please send someone else to do it!" (Ex 4:13). But God's response to all of his servants—including you—is essentially the same: "My grace is sufficient for you" (2 Cor 12:9).

There is another reason you should feel encouraged. Leading a Bible discussion is not difficult if you follow certain guidelines. You don't need to be an expert on the Bible or a trained teacher. The suggestions listed below should enable you to effectively and enjoyably fulfill your role as leader.

Using Caring People Bible Studies

Where should you begin? A good starting place is *Handbook for Caring People.* This short book helps develop some basic caring skills like listening to and communicating to people who are in pain. Additionally, it will help you understand the stages that people in grief go through and how to help people who are suffering. Most of all, this book shows how to rely on God for the strength you need to care for others. At the end of each chapter, you'll find questions for individual or group use.

For the next step you might choose *Resources for Caring People* or *The*

Character of Caring People. Resources for Caring People will show how God empowers us to serve others through Scripture, prayer, the Holy Spirit and many other gifts. *The Character of Caring People* shows what the heart of the Christian caregiver is like. The concerns which emerge within the group during the studies will provide you with guidance for what to do next. All of the guides give help and encouragement to those who want to care for others, but different groups may find some guides more useful than others.

You might want to focus on specific concerns like *Caring for People in Grief* or *Caring for People in Conflict.* Or your group might choose to study topics which reflect areas they need to grow in. For instance, those who have sick friends or relatives or who simply want to be more sensitive to the physical needs that are all around us will find *Caring for Physical Needs* helpful. Others may want to know more about the spiritual concerns people have. *Caring for Spiritual Needs* is a great resource for this. For a biblical perspective on how God wants us to deal with emotional problems, you might choose *Caring for Emotional Needs.* The key is to remember that we all have these needs. Our physical condition affects us spiritually and emotionally. A spiritual problem can have physical and emotional consequences. By covering several of these guides in sequence, members of your group will develop a complete picture of what it means to be a caring Christian.

Preparing for the Study

1. Ask God to help you understand and apply the passage in your own life. Unless this happens, you will not be prepared to lead others. Pray too for the various members of the group. Ask God to open your hearts to the message of his Word and to motivate you to action.

2. Read the introduction to the entire guide to get an overview of the subject at hand and the issues which will be explored.

3. As you begin each study, read and reread the assigned Bible passage to familiarize yourself with it.

4. This study guide is based on the New International Version of the Bible. It will help you and the group if you use this translation as the basis for your study and discussion.

5. Carefully work through each question in the study. Spend time in med-

itation and reflection as you consider how to respond.

6. Write your thoughts and responses in the space provided in the study guide. This will help you to express your understanding of the passage clearly.

7. It might help you to have a Bible dictionary handy. Use it to look up any unfamiliar words, names or places. (For additional help on how to study a passage, see chapter five of *Leading Bible Discussions*, IVP.)

8. Take the response portion of each study seriously. Consider what this means for your life—what changes you might need to make in your lifestyle and/or actions you need to take in the world. Remember that the group will follow your lead in responding to the studies.

Leading the Study

1. Begin the study on time. Open with prayer, asking God to help the group to understand and apply the passage.

2. Be sure that everyone in your group has a study guide. Encourage the group to prepare beforehand for each discussion by reading the introduction to the guide and by working through the questions in the study.

3. At the beginning of your first time together, explain that these studies are meant to be discussions, not lectures. Encourage the members of the group to participate. However, do not put pressure on those who may be hesitant to speak during the first few sessions.

4. Have a group member read the introductory paragraph at the beginning of the discussion. This will orient the group to the topic of the study.

5. Every study begins with an "approach" question, which is meant to be asked before the passage is read. These questions are important for several reasons.

First, there is always a stiffness that needs to be overcome before people will begin to talk openly. A good question will break the ice.

Second, most people will have lots of different things going on in their minds (dinner, an important meeting coming up, how to get the car fixed) that will have nothing to do with the study. A creative question will get their attention and draw them into the discussion.

Third, approach questions can reveal where our thoughts or feelings need to be transformed by Scripture. That is why it is especially important not to read the passage before the approach question is asked. The passage will tend to color the honest reactions people would otherwise give because they are, of course, supposed to think the way the Bible does.

6. Have a group member read aloud the passage to be studied.

7. As you ask the questions, keep in mind that they are designed to be used just as they are written. You may simply read them aloud. Or you may prefer to express them in your own words. There may be times when it is appropriate to deviate from the study guide. For example, a question may have already been answered. If so, move on to the next question. Or someone may raise an important question not covered in the guide. Take time to discuss it, but try to keep the group from going off on tangents.

8. Avoid answering your own questions. If necessary, repeat or rephrase them until they are clearly understood. An eager group quickly becomes passive and silent if they think the leader will do most of the talking.

9. Don't be afraid of silence. People may need time to think about the question before formulating their answers.

10. Don't be content with just one answer. Ask, "What do the rest of you think?" or "Anything else?" until several people have given answers to the question.

11. Acknowledge all contributions. Try to be affirming whenever possible. Never reject an answer. If it is clearly off-base, ask, "Which verse led you to that conclusion?" or again, "What do the rest of you think?"

12. Don't expect every answer to be addressed to you, even though this will probably happen at first. As group members become more at ease, they will begin to truly interact with each other. This is one sign of healthy discussion.

13. Don't be afraid of controversy. It can be very stimulating. If you don't resolve an issue completely, don't be frustrated. Move on and keep it in mind for later. A subsequent study may solve the problem.

14. Periodically summarize what the group has said about the passage. This helps to draw together the various ideas mentioned and gives continuity to the study. But don't preach.

15. Don't skip over the response questions. It's important that we not lose the focus of helping others even as we reflect on ourselves. Be willing to get things started by describing how you have been affected by the study.

16. Conclude your time together with conversational prayer. Ask for God's help in following through on the commitments you've made.

17. End on time. Many more suggestions and helps are found in *Small Group Leader's Handbook* and *Good Things Come in Small Groups* (both from IVP). Reading through one of these books would be worth your time.

Listening to Emotional Pain

Caring People Bible Studies are designed to take seriously the pain and struggle that is part of life. People will experience a variety of emotions during these studies. Keep in mind that you are not expected to act as a professional counselor. However, part of your role as group leader may be to listen to emotional pain. Listening is a gift which you can give to a person who is hurting. For many people, it is not an easy gift to give. The following suggestions will help you to listen more effectively to people in emotional pain.

1. Remember that you are not responsible to take the pain away. People in helping relationships often feel that they are being asked to make the other person feel better. This may be related to the helper not being comfortable with painful feelings.

2. Not only are you not responsible to take the pain away, one of the things people need most is an opportunity to face and to experience the pain in their lives. Many have spent years denying their pain and running from it. Healing can come when we are able to face our pain in the presence of someone who cares about us. Rather than trying to take the pain away, then, commit yourself to listening attentively as it is expressed.

3. Realize that some group members may not feel comfortable with others' expressions of sadness or anger. You may want to acknowledge that such emotions are uncomfortable, but say that learning to feel our own pain is often the first step in helping others with their pain.

4. Be very cautious about giving answers and advice. Advice and answers may make you feel better or feel competent, but they may also minimize people's problems and their painful feelings. Simple solutions rarely work, and they can easily communicate "You should be better now" or "You shouldn't really be talking about this."

5. Be sure to communicate direct affirmation any time people talk about their painful emotions. It takes courage to talk about our pain because it creates anxiety for us. It is a great gift to be trusted by those who are struggling. The following notes refer to specific questions in the study:

Study 1. Called to Care. Isaiah 61:1-3.
Purpose: To hear and respond to Jesus' call to care for others.
Question 2. It is clear that the main figure in this passage is the Messianic servant. Jesus reads this passage and then announces that it is fulfilled in their hearing (Lk 4:17-21). Because we are his disciples, his call becomes our call to ministry. Help the group to look carefully at who Jesus was to minister to and how he was to do it. This will increase their understanding of their own ministry and call to care for others.
Question 3. You need to keep in mind that a very literal interpretation of this passage is in order. Jesus preached good news to the poor and will ultimately bring release to captives. The passage also has a deep figurative meaning in that people are imprisoned by many things such as sin or emotional needs. Many are poor spiritually. Some are in great darkness due to such things as grief or loneliness. Look closely at the different categories of people and the kind of ministry that is involved in caring for them. Be specific and practical.
Question 5. Help lead the group to consider the necessity of responding to God's call to care for others. Help provide an environment in which people can express fears and anxieties about caring as well as excitement and awareness of the cost.
Question 7. Thinking about an oak tree and its characteristics will help give a vision for what the needy people in our lives can become as we care for them. How rapidly do oak trees grow? What happens to their roots? What are they like when they are full grown? What kind of care do they need in order to grow?
Question 8. It excites me to know that people with whom I am privileged to share the good news will, in time, become oaks of righteousness, plantings of the Lord for the display of his splendor! As I consider the oak, I realize that time and energy are involved. Growth does not happen overnight. Sometimes long periods of time can go by without my seeing any growth. Yet the

final outcome is well worth it.

Question 9. This is not a duplicate of question 6, but a specific application of it. What could be the specific and practical end results of your ministry in this person's life?

Study 2. Faith. Genesis 22:1-19.

Purpose: To consider the importance of faith in the life of the caring person.

Question 2. As a leader be prepared to share a situation in which your attitude toward God was like Abraham's. At times people hesitate to share what they are doing right because they fear sounding proud.

Question 3. If we want to understand this passage, it helps to put ourselves in Abraham's shoes. Encourage the members of the group to enter into Abraham's dilemma as much as possible.

Question 4. Hebrews 11 is the biblical hall of fame for those who had faith. Abraham is one of the patriarchs listed in that chapter. In fact, more is said about him then any other person. The definition of faith is also found there.

Question 6. One definition of faith is found in Hebrews 11. Faith can also be defined as trusting what God says is true and acting accordingly. Faith without obedience is empty. Take time to look closely at how Abraham demonstrated his faith by his obedience.

Questions 11. In faith, as in most aspects of the Christian life, there is a delicate balance to maintain. There are times when we need to see God work now, and faith requires that we believe him for that. There are times too when we are called on to wait. The patriarchs in Hebrews 11 did not receive the things that they were promised, but they saw them and welcomed them from a distance. God's view and plan is so much greater than we are. Discuss freely and openly the tension that this can cause us.

Study 3. Hope. Colossians 1:15-29.

Purpose: To grow as a person of hope as a result of looking at Jesus Christ who is our source of hope.

Question 2. According to *Webster's Dictionary*, supreme means: "1. highest in rank, power, authority, etc. dominant. 2. highest in quality, achievement, etc. most excellent. 3. highest in degree, utmost. 4. final, ultimate."

This passage is a rich description of Jesus Christ. Help the group to appreciate his supremacy by looking thoroughly at these verses.

Question 3. Jesus is the image of his Father. He makes it possible for us to see God. "It is because man bore God's image that it was possible for God to become man. In this way what otherwise would be invisible becomes visible to man" (D. Guthrie, J. A. Motyer, A. M. Stibbs, D. J. Wiseman, eds., *The New Bible Commentary: Revised* [Grand Rapids, Mich.: Eerdmans, 1973], p. 1143).

The son is the only perfect representation of God. Men may make images of God but in so doing they deface the glory of the incorruptible God. But in Christ God's glory is not defaced but perfectly seen. Just as the image on the coin is the true copy of the head of the sovereign, or just as a child shows a marked likeness to a parent, so Christ in a deeper way is the perfect revelation to men of the invisible God. The unique revelation of God given by the son is clearly and fully declared. God dwells in light inaccessible, and may not be seen by human eyes, but in the son we may see his true likeness. (R. V. G. Tasker, gen. ed., *The Epistles of Paul to the Colossians and Philemon* [Grand Rapids, Mich: Eerdmans, 1979], p. 42.)

By stating that the fullness of God dwells in Christ, Paul is saying that all of God's essence and power dwells in Christ. This expresses the highest possible view of Christ. It is also clear by the context that God was pleased for this to happen; that is, he was pleased by the Incarnation.

Question 5. "It is Jesus' resurrection, the emergence of life victorious over death, which establishes His title to be the source of Life. But since He was the first to be so raised, the resurrection also established his primacy over those who should experience a like resurrection. There is no contradiction here involved in stating that He is the 'firstborn from the dead', and in accepting the raising of Lazarus or any other such miracles in Scripture. Lazarus was raised to his former corruptible condition, and was still liable to death; but the Son was raised incorruptible, never to taste of death again" (*The Epistles of Paul,* p. 44).

Question 7. Your discussion should focus on Jesus as the center of our hope because of what he did for us.

Study 4. Love. Luke 10:25-42.
Purpose: To learn what it means to love God and to love others.
Question 3. We can learn a lot about people just by observing their conversations. As a group, try to find out as much as you can about what the expert in the law is like.
Question 4. Discover ways that group members are like the lawyer in their relationships with Jesus. For instance, when do they try, overtly or subconsciously, to "test God"? Or do they know what Scripture says, but fail to apply it? Do they sometimes defend themselves for disobedience? As you discuss application, make sure the discussion continues around the subject of loving others. For instance, when do we fail to act on what we know about the two greatest commandments? How is testing God a sign of not loving and trusting him? When have group members done this? What does loving God have to do with loving others?
Question 5. The priest and Levite may have feared ritual defilement by touching a corpse. The fact that Jesus used a Samaritan as the person who showed love and who was the neighbor, makes the story more powerful. The Jews hated the Samaritans. It is possible that in verse 37 the Jewish lawyer could not even bring himself to say "the Samaritan" in answer to Jesus' question, "Which of these three do you think was a neighbor to the man who fell into the hands of the robbers?"

It is worth noting that the priest and Levite were heading *down* the road; that is, they were headed not for Jerusalem and the temple (where their services might be required) but for Jericho.
Question 7. Try to lead the group beyond talking just about what the Samaritan did. Also look at what it cost him, and the implications of each of his acts. Think about where he could have stopped in his care, but instead how he continued. He not only risked his reputation with his own people by being associated with a Jew, he gave up his time to get him to the inn. The Samaritan planned for the man's future as well as his present by promising to pay for all expenses that might occur.
Question 9. The responses may not be either/or, but a combination of each.
Question 10. Help the group to consider "what is needed" from both Jesus and Mary's perspectives.

Question 13. This question is designed not only to help the group to apply the material that has been studied, but to prepare them for praying for each other, as suggested in the last question. Prayer is an important part of each study.

It should also be noted that when Jesus said, "Mary has chosen what is better," he meant that Mary needed to learn from him, to sit at his feet as his disciple. However, a legitimate secondary interpretation is that Mary did indeed show love to Jesus by attentive listening. Jesus was man as well as God; it seems very reasonable to think that he was affected positively and felt cared for by Mary's quiet listening.

Study 5. Generosity. 2 Corinthians 9:6-15.

Purpose: To consider biblical principles of generosity so that we can integrate them into our lives.

Question 2. By "intentional" giving, I mean making plans for our giving. As in the rest of our financial planning, our giving should be thought through and the plan should be stuck to. This needs to be seen as a commitment to God and followed through.

We are to give intentionally, first, out of obedience to God who asks for a portion of our income. Second, intentional giving is necessary so that priorities can be established, and money is carefully used so that giving will not be pushed aside. Additionally, we give so that folk in full-time Christian service know that they can depend on those who have committed to their support. Finally, it leaves room for the more spontaneous giving when new needs are brought to our attention.

Question 3. The main reason is that a positive attitude pleases God for "God loves a cheerful giver." Also our joy, and possibly that of the recipient, is diminished by reluctant giving that is done with grudging.

Question 4. You as the leader could be very helpful here in creating an environment in which people can grow through being vulnerable. If you have examples from your own experience, it would help to share them.

However, not everyone struggles with this. Do not feel that you have to relate negative experiences if you have none. If you sense that you have a group of people who love to give or who long to obey God in this area, move on to the next question or direct the question to difficulties in deciding what is right to give, whether it is right for Christians to save money, and so forth. People who are serious about giving struggle with some of these issues, especially those of us who live in the West and have so much.

Question 5. "Generous giving for those who have little to give seems very hazardous; but the risk tends to be forgotten when the greatness of God's power is kept steadily in mind. All our resources, great or small, come ultimately from God; and *God is able*, Paul insists, to increase those resources. Where the generous spirit exists, God will provide the means by which it can be expressed. *Grace* is used here concretely; so RSV 'provide you with every blessing in abundance'. The result is that, furnished with the ability that God can supply, the charitable man will *always* have *all sufficiency in all things*. The word translated *sufficiency, autorkeia,* means first 'self sufficiency', the feeling of being able to rely on one's own resources without having to look to others or, as the Stoics said, without being dependent on the caprices of fortune; and secondly, it describes the contentment which such self-sufficiency engenders. . . . Here the apostle states that the believer by divine grace is ·rendered self-sufficient and competent to meet the demands made on his generosity, so that he *may abound to every good work,* i.e. to be able to perform it" (R. V. G. Tasker, *The Second Epistle of Paul to the Corinthians,* Tyndale New Testament Commentaries [Grand Rapids, Mich.: Eerdmans, 1978], pp. 126-27).

Question 9. Your giving supplies the needs of God's people, causes expressions of thanks to God to overflow, confirms your commitment to the gospel, and encourages prayer on your behalf.

Study 6. Encouragement. Hebrews 10:19-25.

Purpose: To understand the connection between the confidence that we have in our faith and encouragement. To strive to become a more encouraging person.

Question 2. As you work through this passage ask God to make real the confidence that we have in Jesus' sacrifice for us, in being a part of God's household and in his role as a faithful high priest. Ask him to make you very grateful that you not only should but can draw near to God in full assurance of faith. These realities are the basis for encouraging one another. Help your group to see the connection, relate what encouragement has meant to them and think through what it means in a practical day-to-day sense to become an encouraging person.

A curtain in the temple covered up the Holy of Holies. It was out of the people's view. Once a year on the Day of Atonement, only the high priest could enter so that he could atone for the nation's sins. But all believers may now walk right into God's presence because Jesus' death has removed the curtain and opened up the way to God.

"The effectiveness of . . . Christ's work is now shown to lie in the liberty of the believer to enter God's presence in contrast to those under the old covenant who had not direct access to God; and even the privilege granted to the high priest to approach Him on their behalf was confined to one day a year. The believer can approach the holiest not only without fear and trembling but with full assurance that by *the blood of Jesus,* i.e. in virtue of Christ's better sacrifice, he will be graciously received by the Father.

"His death, as it were, uncovered God so that man might have a vision of the glory that shone upon His face" (R. V. G. Tasker, *The Epistle to the Hebrews,* Tyndale New Testament Commentaries [Grand Rapids, Mich.: Eerdmans, 1979], pp. 160-61).

Question 3. This question is meant to prepare the way for the next question concerning our response to God. In talking about human relationships my hope is that the openness that we have with God because of the offenses being settled may be more deeply appreciated.

Question 4. Intimacy with God is a precious gift. In order to have this intimacy we *should* draw near to God with a sincere heart in full assurance. We do need to accept Jesus' work for ourselves and we need to believe him. But we also *get* to draw near in intimacy and in full assurance.

Question 5. "In the face of temptations to abandon their confidence because some promises remained unfulfilled, the writer appeals for a steadfast persistence in openly confessing their Christian hope; for they have the guarantee of the faithfulness of the Promiser" (Donald Guthrie, gen. ed., *The New Bible Commentary: Revised* [Grand Rapids, Mich.: Eerdmans, 1973], p. 1209).

Help the group to talk through practical ways of "holding to the hope." For instance, saturating themselves with the truth of Scripture, prayer, praying and sharing with others, talking about God's work in lives and in the world.

Study 7. Hospitality. 1 Peter 4:7-11.
Purpose. To recognize that hospitality is an important aspect of the character of the caring person and to consider what hospitality is and how to grow as a hospitable person.
Question 3. "They should also know that the true fulfilment of their calling and destiny in Christ lies beyond death and the present world-order, in a 'salvation ready to be revealed in the last time' (1.5), at 'the appearing of Jesus Christ' (1.7). This earthly life in the flesh, and this present age are not to go on for ever. There are to be both a termination and a consummation of *all things.* Also, this inevitable *end is at hand.* It is always to be thought of as impending. This awareness should disturb their complacency, and make them face daily living with a new sense of eternal values. It provides a further reason for abandoning a life of self-indulgence, and for practicing self-discipline, prayer and loving service, of the brethren" (R. V. G. Tasker, ed., *The First Epistle General of Peter,* The Tyndale New Testament Commentaries [Grand Rapids, Mich.: Eerdmans, 1979], p. 153).
Question 4. *"Be ye therefore sober, or 'of sound mind'.* The verb *sophronein,* 'to be in one's right mind', 'in control of oneself', is used to describe the restored demoniac at Gadara (Mark v. 15). It is also used in contrast both to being 'beside oneself' or 'mad' (2 Cor. v. 13), and to 'thinking too highly of oneself' (Rom. xii. 3). There are dangers to spiritual well-being in intemperance, uncontrolled excitement or frenzy, and conceit. This sinful and self-indulgent world is not the place to lose one's mental or moral balance. Those who would be ready for Christ's appearing should keep their head and conscience clear.

"*Watch unto prayer,* or be 'sober unto prayers' enforces the same exhortation for the added reason that such sobriety is indispensable to full prayerfulness. Christians must not allow their minds to become fuddled by drink or drowsiness. They should keep themselves awake and alert, with all their faculties under control, in order to be able to give themselves to praying. Peter possibly had in mind here the way in which in the Garden of Gethsemane he failed to pray because he went to sleep and failed to watch. As a result, he was unprepared to withstand temptation (see Mark xiv. 37-40, 66-72)" (Tasker, *Peter*, pp. 153-54).

Question 6. "Another way in which Christian love may find active practical expression is in showing *hospitality* to Christians from other places, who as strangers or visitors are personally unknown, but who need shelter and food. By becoming Christians many ceased to enjoy the welcome and help of former potential friends. They stood, therefore, in urgent need of compensating Christian friendship at the hands of those who were now their brethren in Christ" (Tasker, *Peter*, pp. 153-55).

Question 7. You may want to read the following excerpt concerning hospitality to help your group develop the broad scope of hospitality and what it means to practice it. You as the leader need to begin with a broad picture. You might even want to read parts of this to the group after they have finished responding to this question and you feel a greater concept is needed. Certainly use your interpretation of the following information in guiding the group through the discussion of this question. All the rest of the study depends on this concept.

In the *Disciplemakers' Handbook* Alice Fryling describes hospitality in the following way:

"My experience with hospitality is that it comes in three forms: extensive sharing of your home and life, entertaining visitors and relational hospitality.

"The first kind of hospitality is the kind that my friends Joanne and Julie practice. They regularly invite people to stay in their apartment for extended periods of time. Their home is a drop-in spot for students who live nearby. Their dinner table always has room for one more. Extensive hospitality like this is indeed a gift of the Spirit.

"The second form of hospitality is probably the most familiar to us. It is the invitation-to-dinner kind of hospitality. We give to our guests not just a meal but the experience of a pleasant time in our home. This kind of hospitality is important as a building block in relationships, but it should not become the end of our hospitable efforts. . . .

"Hospitality, finally, is a welcoming of someone into your life and into your heart and mind. Even without physical touch, it is an embracing with words and curiosity that touch another's heart. I often try to extend hospitality to waitresses and sales clerks by taking a moment to ask them something about their work. I extend hospitality to my friend by calling and saying, 'I just wanted to know what your day is like.' And, of course, sometimes I extend hospitality in my home with a meal or a cup of tea.

"But it is deceptive to think that just because someone is in my home I am being hospitable in the relational sense. During a weekend conference once, I was assigned housing with a Christian family in the area. I happened to stay with them on the night of their favorite TV show. From the time I arrived until I went to bed, we watched television. They may have thought they were being hospitable by housing me during the conference, but in fact what they gave me was merely bed and board.

"To understand the fullest meaning of hospitality, think of life as being made up of hosts and guests. The hosts of life are the ones who are available to listen, who offer compassion by being genuine and honest about themselves and who invite you to feel at home, wherever you are. The guests are those who respond. They are the ones who receive acceptance, peace, stimulation and love from the hosts" (Alice Fryling, *Disciplemakers' Handbook* [Downers Grove, Ill.: InterVarsity Press, 1989], pp. 79-80).

Being a caring person means opening up our lives to those who are in need of Christ's love and of our love.

Some specific ways of practicing hospitality are introducing yourself when a new person comes into a group you are in, asking people questions about themselves in an effort to get to know them better, inquiring about how life is going for people in your life, listening actively to people's responses to your question, giving hugs when appropriate and comfortable, taking risks in sharing yourself and being vulnerable with others, making your home a haven and place of welcome, and writing notes of gratitude and affirmation. Ask God to show you creative ways of living out hospitality by welcoming people into your life.

Question 8. "The insertion of the phrase *without grumbling,* implies that the demands on some of showing such hospitality were frequent and heavy, and that naturally they might have been tempted to be resentful and complaining. But such opportunities of showing love to Christian brethren in need ought to be gladly embraced as a Christian privilege, and indeed a form of service to Christ Himself" (Tasker, *Peter,* p. 155).

Study 8. Accepting Our Limits. Exodus 18:13-24.

Purpose: To understand the necessity of our being aware of our limits even as we strive to please God and to care for others.

Question 4. This is a speculative question and is meant to get your group members into the passage. Lead the group to discuss what he might have been feeling in relation to the job, to his father-in-law's involvement, to sharing his leadership and hence giving up some power, to trusting others to help in the task. The sky is the limit on what you might discuss. It prepares your group for the next question of identifying with Moses and how they each feel about their involvements.

Question 5. Many times we feel that people we minister to and the things we need to do are around us from morning to evening. We take on more than we can possibly do. Help group members to get into this passage through this question.

Question 9. Be sure to discuss how willing members of the group are to listen to others who are concerned and wise and instruments of God.

Question 10. One benefit is that Moses did not, to use modern terminology, "burn out." A second benefit was that tension between his father-in-law and himself did not develop because Moses did not resist the truth his father-in-law spoke. Third, Moses was able to "disciple" others and see God's work through them. Those under him who were given this responsibility would have grown a lot in the process. Finally, the people who needed help got more prompt and satisfying attention.

About the Author

Phyllis J. Le Peau is a registered nurse and a former Nurses Christian Fellowship staffworker. Currently, she is assistant program director for Wellness, Inc. Phyllis is also the author of the Fruit of the Spirit Bible Studies Kindness, Gentleness and Joy *(Zondervan) and coauthor of* Disciplemakers' Handbook *(IVP). With her husband, Andy, she has coauthored* One Plus One Equals One *and the LifeGuide® Bible Studies* Ephesians *and* James *(IVP/SU). She and her husband live in Downers Grove, Illinois, with their four children.*

Caring People Bible Studies from InterVarsity Press
By Phyllis J. Le Peau

Handbook for Caring People (coauthored by Bonnie J. Miller). This book provides simple, time-tested principles for dealing with the pain, the questions and the crises people face. You will get the basic tools for communication plus some practical suggestions. Questions for group discussion are at the end of each chapter.

Resources for Caring People. Through God, we have the resources we need to help others. God has given us Scripture, prayer, the Holy Spirit, listening and acceptance. This guide will show you how he works through people like you every day. 8 studies.

The Character of Caring People. The key to caring is character. These Bible studies will show you how to focus on the gifts of caring which God has given you—such as hospitality, generosity and encouragement. 8 studies.

Caring for Spiritual Needs. A relationship with God. Meaning and purpose. Belonging. Love. Assurance. These are just some of the spiritual needs that we all have. This Bible study guide will help you learn how these needs can be met in your life and in the lives of others. 9 studies.

Caring for Emotional Needs. We think we have to act like we have it all together, yet sometimes we are lonely, afraid or depressed. Christians have emotional needs just like everyone else. This Bible study guide shows how to find emotional health for ourselves and how to help others. 9 studies.

Caring for Physical Needs. When we are sick or when our basic needs for food, clothing and adequate housing are not being met, our whole being—body, spirit and emotion—is affected. When we care for the physical needs of others, we are showing God's love. These Bible studies will help you learn to do that. 8 studies.

Caring for People in Conflict. Divided churches. Broken friendships. Angry children. Torn marriages. We all have to deal with conflict and the emotions which accompany it. These studies will show you how God can bring healing and reconciliation. 9 studies.

Caring for People in Grief. Because sin brought death into the world, we all have to look into death's ugly face at one time or another. These Bible studies cover the issues which consume those who are grieving—fear, peace, grace and hope—and show you how to provide them with comfort. 9 studies.